THE

PRIVATE DEVOTIONS

OF

LANCELOT ANDREWES

THE

PRIVATE DEVOTIONS

OF

LANCELOT ANDREWES

*Translated from the Greek and
Arranged Anew by*

JOHN HENRY NEWMAN

New York   Nashville
ABINGDON-COKESBURY PRESS

Copyright 1950 by Pierce and Smith
PRINTED IN THE UNITED STATES OF AMERICA

Publisher's Foreword

THE devotions of Lancelot Andrewes belong to the timeless literature of Christianity. Although written for himself alone, and reflecting here and there his personal interests and the spirit of his time, they express the deepest feelings of the devout Christian in every generation.

The man who wrote these prayers was a Christian leader of prominence in his time (1555-1626). He served three years as chaplain to Queen Elizabeth, became canon of St. Paul's, and was dean of Westminster Abbey when the new king invited him to the conference at which the King James Version of the Bible was proposed. In this project he was made chairman of the committee responsible for translating the first section of the Old Testament—Genesis through Kings. Meanwhile he was consecrated bishop of Chichester in 1605 and later served the dioceses of Ely and Winchester. During the latter years of his life he was a member of the Privy Council, dean of the Chapel Royal, and more than once an adviser of the king.

It is through his little book of personal prayers, however, rather than his statesmanlike acts, that Lancelot Andrewes yet lives. Written in Greek, these prayers were never meant for the eyes of others—as may be seen in certain intimate references to his family, his diocese, and the England of his day. A few years after his death English translations of portions were published, but it was not until 1675 that the Oxford Press brought out the first complete edition, in the original Greek. Since then the book has gone through edition after edition all over the world.

Among a number of English translations the most beautiful is that of John Henry Newman, literary genius and eminent churchman of Victorian days. He prepared the translation for publication in his *Tracts for the Times* in 1840, at the height of his leadership in the controversial Oxford Movement. The devotional richness of Andrewes' prayers completely smothered any polemic purposes of the translator, however, and only the historian can discover what those purposes were. Hence, as Newman notes in his "Advertisement," the work was reissued as a simple devotional book in 1842 under the title *The Devotions of Bishop Andrewes*.

Today the reader of these prayers is hardly conscious of the doctrinal or political issues of past centuries that moved author and translator. Rather he finds in them a guide to personal communion with the God in whom both found strength for their day. This new edition, produced by photographing a limited edition now long out of print, is presented that once again the rare and timeless quality of these devotions may be available to Christian hearts and homes.

Advertisement

THE following Translation of the Greek Devotions of Bishop Andrewes is made from the Edition of 1675, and has already appeared in a publication of the day. It is reprinted in its present form in compliance with the suggestion of many persons, who naturally wished to possess it simply as a devotional work, apart from its controversial bearings. A few alterations have been made in the arrangement of its separate parts, as they occur in the present text of the original, but only with a view to its answering more fully the purpose for which it seems to have been composed, of furnishing a manual of devotion for every day of the week. Accordingly, such portions of the work, as were obviously without or out of place, have been inserted, where they were wanted, in the course of the prayers ; or collected together at the end ; or, if repetitions, omitted. No alterations have been made in the text itself; and all transpositions are noted at the foot of the page, as they occur.

J. H. N.

Feast of All Saints.

Contents

Daily Prayers

Preparation

1. *Times of Prayer*

Always. *Luke* xviii. 1.

Without ceasing. 1 *Thes.* v. 17.

At all times. *Eph.* vi. 18.

Samuel among such as call upon His name[a]. *Ps.* xcix. 6.

God forbid that I should sin against the Lord in ceasing to pray for you, and shewing you the good and the right way. 1 *Sam.* xii. 23.

We will give ourselves continually to prayer and to the ministry of the word. *Acts* vi. 4.

He kneeled upon his knees three times a day, and prayed and gave thanks before his God, as he did aforetime. *Dan.* vi. 10.

In the evening, and morning, and at noon day will I pray, and that instantly, and He shall hear my voice. *Ps.* lv. 18.

[a] Transferred from p. 4 of Edition of 1675.

Seven times a day do I praise Thee. *Ps.* cxix. 164.

1. In the morning, a great while before day. *Mark* i. 35.

2. In the morning watch. *Ps.* lxiii. 6. [vid. also *Ps.* cxxx. 6.]

3. The third hour of the day. *Acts* ii. 15.

4. About the sixth hour. *Acts* x. 9.

5. The hour of prayer, the ninth. *Acts* iii. 1.

6. The eventide. *Gen.* xxiv. 63.

7. By night. *Ps.* cxxxiv. 2.

At midnight. *Ps.* cxix. 62.

2. *Places of Prayer*

In all places where I record My Name, I will come to thee, and I will bless thee. *Exod.* xx. 24.

Let [b] Thine eyes be open towards this house night and day, even toward the place of which Thou hast said, My Name shall be there ; that Thou mayest hearken unto the prayer which Thy servant shall make towards this place. 1 *Kings* viii. 29.

Thou that hearest the prayer
unto Thee shall all flesh come.
The fierceness of man shall turn to Thy praise,
and the fierceness of them shalt Thou refrain.

[b] Transferred from pp. 5, 6, and 9, of Edition 1675.

As for me, I will come into Thy house
even upon the multitude of Thy mercy,
and in Thy fear will I worship
toward Thy Holy Temple.
Hear the voice of my humble petitions,
when I cry unto Thee;
when I hold up my hands
towards the mercy-seat of Thy Holy Temple.
We wait for Thy loving-kindness, O God,
in the midst of Thy Temple.

1. Among the faithful and in the congregation. *Ps.* cxi. 1.

2. Enter into thy closet, and, when thou hast shut thy door, pray to thy Father which is in secret. *Matt.* vi. 6.

3. They went up into an upper room. *Acts* i. 13.

4. He went up upon the housetop to pray. *Acts* x. 9.

5. They went up together into the Temple. *Acts* iii. 1.

6. We kneeled down on the shore, and prayed. *Acts* xxi. 5.

7. He went forth over the brook Cedron, where was a garden. *John* xviii. 1.

8. Let them rejoice in their beds. *Ps.* cxlix. 5.

9. He departed into a desert place and there prayed. *Mark* i. 35.

10. In every place lifting up holy hands without wrath and doubting. 1 *Tim.* ii. 8.

3. *Circumstances of Prayer*

1. Kneeling,   *humiliation.*

He kneeled down and prayed. *Luke* xxii. 41.

He went a little further, and fell on His face, and prayed. *Matt.* xxvi. 39.

My soul is brought low, even unto the dust,
     my belly cleaveth unto the ground.

2. Sinking the head,   *shame.*

Drooping the face. [*Ezr.* ix. 6.]

3. Smiting the breast, [*Luke* xviii. 13.]
                     indignation.

4. Shuddering, [*Acts* xvi. 29.] *fear.*

5. Groaning, [*Isai.* lix. 11.] *sorrow.*

Clasping of hands.

6. Raising of eyes and hands, [*Ps.* xxv. 15; cxliii. 6.]
                     vehement desire.

7. Blows, [*Ps.* lxxiii. 14.] *revenge.*

2 Cor. vii. 11.

Order of Matin Prayer

Litany

Glory be to Thee, O Lord, glory to Thee.
Glory to Thee who givest me sleep
to recruit my weakness,
and to remit the toils
of this fretful flesh.
To this day and all days,
a perfect, holy, peaceful, healthy, sinless course,
Vouchsafe O Lord.

The Angel of peace, a faithful guide,
guardian of souls and bodies,
to encamp around me,
and ever to prompt what is salutary,
Vouchsafe O Lord.

Pardon and remission
of all sins and of all offences
Vouchsafe O Lord.

To our souls what is good and convenient,
　　and peace to the world,
　　　　　　　Vouchsafe O Lord.

Repentance and strictness
　for the residue of our life,
and health and peace to the end,
　　　　　　　Vouchsafe O Lord.

Whatever is true, whatever is honest,
　whatever just, whatever pure,
whatever lovely, whatever of good report,
　if there be any virtue, if any praise,
　　such thoughts, such deeds,
　　　　　　　Vouchsafe O Lord.

A Christian close,
　without sin, without shame,
and, should it please Thee, without pain,
　　and a good answer
at the dreadful and fearful judgment-seat
　of Jesus Christ our Lord,
　　　　　　　Vouchsafe O Lord.

Confession

Essence beyond essence, Nature increate,
Framer of the world,
I set Thee, Lord, before my face,
and I lift up my soul unto Thee.
I worship Thee on my knees,
and humble myself under Thy mighty hand.
I stretch forth my hands unto Thee,
my soul gaspeth unto Thee as a thirsty land.
I smite on my breast
and say with the Publican,
God be merciful to me a sinner,
the chief of sinners ;
to the sinner above the Publican,
be merciful as to the Publican.
Father of mercies,
I beseech Thy fatherly affection,
despise me not
an unclean worm, a dead dog, a putrid corpse,
despise not Thou the work of thine own hands,
despise not Thine own image
though branded by sin.

Lord, if Thou wilt, Thou canst make me clean;
Lord, only say the word, and I shall be cleansed.
And Thou, my Saviour Christ,
Christ my Saviour,
Saviour of sinners, of whom I am chief,
despise me not, despise me not, O Lord,
despise not the cost of Thy blood,
who am called by Thy name;
but look on me with those eyes
with which Thou didst look upon
Magdalene at the feast,
Peter in the hall,
the thief on the wood;—
that with the thief I may entreat Thee humbly,
Remember me, Lord, in Thy kingdom;
that with Peter I may bitterly weep and say,
O that mine eyes were a fountain of tears
that I might weep day and night;
that with Magdalene I may hear Thee say,
Thy sins be forgiven thee,
and with her may love much,
for many sins yea manifold
have been forgiven me.
And Thou, All-holy, Good, and Life-giving Spirit,
despise me not, Thy breath,

despise not Thine own holy things ;
but turn Thee again, O Lord, at the last,
and be gracious unto Thy servant.

Commendation

Blessed art Thou, O Lord,
Our God,
the God of our Fathers ;
who turnest the shadow of death into the morning ;
and lightenest the face of the earth ;
who separatest darkness from the face of the light ;
and banishest night and bringest back the day ;
who lightenest mine eyes,
that I sleep not in death ;
who deliverest me from the terror by night,
from the pestilence that walketh in darkness ;
who drivest sleep from mine eyes,
and slumber from mine eyelids ;
who makest the outgoings of the morning and evening
to praise Thee ;
because I laid me down and slept and rose up again,
for the Lord sustained me ;
because I waked and beheld,
and my sleep was sweet unto me.
Blot out as a thick cloud my transgressions,

and as a cloud my sins ;
grant me to be a child of light, a child of the day,
to walk soberly, holily, honestly, as in the day ;
vouchsafe to keep me this day without sin.
Thou who upholdest the falling and liftest the fallen,
let me not harden my heart in provocation,
or temptation or deceitfulness of any sin.
Moreover, deliver me to-day
from the snare of the hunter
and from the noisome pestilence ;
from the arrow that flieth by day,
from the sickness that destroyeth in the noon day.
Defend this day against my evil,
against the evil of this day defend Thou me.
Let not my days be spent in vanity,
nor my years in sorrow.
One day telleth another,
and one night certifieth another.
O let me hear Thy loving-kindness betimes in the
morning,
for in Thee is my trust ;
shew Thou me the way that I should walk in,
for I lift up my soul unto Thee.
Deliver me, O Lord, from mine enemies,
for I flee unto Thee.

Teach me to do the thing that pleaseth Thee,
for Thou art my God ;
Let Thy loving Spirit lead me forth
into the land of righteousness.
Quicken me, O Lord, for Thy Name's sake,
and for Thy righteousness' sake
bring my soul out of trouble ;
remove from me foolish imaginations,
inspire those which are good
and pleasing in Thy sight.
Turn away mine eyes
lest they behold vanity ;
let mine eyes look right on,
and let mine eyelids look straight before me.
Hedge up mine ears with thorns
lest they incline to undisciplined words.
Give me early the ear to hear,
and open mine ears to the instruction of Thy oracles.
Set a watch, O Lord, before my mouth,
and keep the door of my lips.
Let my word be seasoned with salt,
that it may minister grace to the hearers.
Let no need be grief unto me
nor offence of heart.
Let me do some work

for which Thou wilt remember me, Lord, for good,
and spare me according to the greatness of Thy mercy.
Into Thine hands I commend
my spirit, soul, and body,
which Thou hast created, redeemed, regenerated,
O Lord, Thou God of truth ;
and together with me
all mine and all that belongs to me.
Thou hast vouchsafed them to me,
Lord, in Thy goodness.
Guard us from all evil,
guard our souls,
I beseech Thee, O Lord.
Guard us without falling,
and place us immaculate
in the presence of Thy glory
in that day.
Guard my going out and my coming in
henceforth and for ever.
Prosper, I pray Thee, Thy servant this day,
and grant him mercy
in the sight of those who meet him.
O God, make speed to save me,
O Lord, make haste to help me.
O turn Thee then unto me,

and have mercy upon me;
give Thy strength unto Thy servant,
and help the son of Thine handmaid.
Shew some token upon me for good,
that they who hate me may see it and be ashamed,
because Thou, Lord, hast holpen me
and comforted me.

Order of Evening Prayer[a]

Meditation

The day is gone,
and I give Thee thanks, O Lord.
Evening is at hand,
make it bright unto us.
As day has its evening
so also has life;
the even of life is age,
age has overtaken me,
make it bright unto us.
Cast me not away in the time of age;
forsake me not when my strength faileth me.
Even to my old age be Thou He,
and even to hoar hairs carry me;
do Thou make, do Thou bear,
do Thou carry and deliver me.

[a] Page 196, edit. 1675.

Abide with me, Lord,
for it is toward evening,
and the day is far spent
of this fretful life.
Let Thy strength be made perfe
in my weakness.

Day is fled and gone,
life too is going,
this lifeless life.
Night cometh,
and cometh death,
the deathless death.
Near as is the end of day,
so too the end of life:
We then, also remembering it,
beseech of Thee
for the close of our life,
that Thou wouldest direct it in peace,
Christian, acceptable,
sinless, shameless,
and, if it please Thee, painless,
Lord, O Lord,
gathering us together
under the feet of Thine Elect,

when Thou wilt, and as Thou wilt,
only without shame and sins.
Remember we the days of darkness,
for they shall be many,
lest we be cast into outer darkness.
Remember we to outstrip the night
doing some good thing.
Near is judgment;—
a good and acceptable answer
at the dreadful and fearful judgment-seat
of Jesus Christ
vouchsafe to us, O Lord.
By night I lift up my hands in the sanctuary,
and praise the Lord.
The Lord hath granted His loving-kindness
in the day time;
and in the night season did I sing of Him,
and made my prayer unto the God of my life.
As long as I live will I magnify Thee on this manner
and lift up my hands in Thy Name.
Let my prayer be set forth in Thy sight
as the incense,
and let the lifting up of my hands
be an evening sacrifice.
Blessed art Thou, O Lord, our God,

the God of our fathers,
who hast created the changes of days and nights,
who givest songs in the night,
who hast delivered us from the evil of this day,
who hast not cut off like a weaver my life,
nor from day even to night made an end of me.

Confession
Lord,
as we add day to day
so sin to sin.
The just falleth seven times a day;
and I, an exceeding sinner,
seventy times seven;
a wonderful, a horrible thing, O Lord.
But I turn with groans
from my evil ways,
and I return into my heart,
and with all my heart I turn to Thee,
O God of penitents and Saviour of sinners;
and evening by evening I will return
in the innermost marrow of my soul;
and my soul out of the deep
crieth unto Thee.
I have sinned, O Lord, against Thee,

heavily against Thee ;
alas, alas, woe is me ! for my misery.
I repent, O me ! I repent, spare me, O Lord,
I repent, O me, I repent,
help Thou my impenitence.
Be appeased, spare me, O Lord ;
be appeased, have mercy on me ;
I said, Lord, have mercy upon me,
heal my soul, for I have sinned against Thee.
Have mercy upon me, O Lord,
after Thy great goodness,
according to the multitude of Thy mercies
do away mine offences.
Remit the guilt,
heal the wound,
blot out the stains,
clear away the shame,
rescue from the tyranny,
and make me not a public example.
O bring Thou me out of my trouble,
cleanse Thou me from secret fault,
keep back Thy servant also from presumptuous sins.
My wanderings of mind
and idle talking
lay not to my charge.

Remove the dark and muddy flood
of foul and wicked thoughts.
O Lord,
I have destroyed myself;
whatever I have done amiss, pardon mercifully.
Deal not with us after our sins,
neither reward us after our iniquities.
Look mercifully upon our infirmities;
and for the glory of Thy All-holy Name,
turn from us all those ills and miseries,
which by our sins, and by us through them
are most righteously and worthily deserved.

Commendation

To my weariness, O Lord,
vouchsafe Thou rest,
to my exhaustion
renew Thou strength.
Lighten mine eyes that I sleep not in death.
Deliver me from the terror by night,
the pestilence that walketh in darkness.
Supply me with healthy sleep,
and to pass through this night without fear.
O keeper of Israel,
who neither slumberest nor sleepest,

guard me this night from all evil,
guard my soul, O Lord.
Visit me with the visitation of Thine own,
reveal to me wisdom in the visions of the night.
If not, for I am not worthy, not worthy,
at least, O loving Lord,
let sleep be to me a breathing time
as from toil, so from sin.
Yea, O Lord,
nor let me in my dreams imagine
what may anger Thee,
what may defile me.
Let not my loins be filled with illusions,
yea, let my reins chasten me in the night season,
yet without grievous terror.
Preserve me from the black sleep of sin ;
all earthly and evil thoughts
put to sleep within me.
Grant to me light sleep,
rid of all imaginations
fleshly and satanical.
Lord, Thou knowest
how sleepless are mine unseen foes,
and how feeble my wretched flesh,
who madest me ;

shelter me with the wing of Thy pity ;
awaken me at the fitting time,
the time of prayer ;
and give me to seek Thee early,
for Thy glory, and for Thy service.

Here use the form of Intercession, No. 3.

Into Thy hands, O Lord, I commend myself,
my spirit, soul, and body :
Thou didst make, and didst redeem them ;
and together with me, all my friends
and all that belongs to me.
Thou hast vouchsafed them to me, Lord,
in Thy goodness.
Guard my lying down and my rising up,
from henceforth and for ever.
Let me remember Thee on my bed,
and search out my spirit;
let me wake up and be present with Thee ;
let me lay me down in peace, and take my rest :
for it is Thou, Lord, only
that makest me dwell in safety.

Course of Prayers for the Week

The First Day

Introduction

Through the tender mercies of our God
the day-spring from on high hath visited us.
Glory be to Thee, O Lord, glory to Thee.
Creator of the light,
and Enlightener of the world,—
of the visible light,
The Sun's ray, a flame of fire,
day and night,
evening and morning,—
of the light invisible,
the revelation of God,
writings of the Law,
oracles of Prophets,
music of Psalms,
instruction of Proverbs,
experience of Histories,—

light which never sets.
God is the Lord who hath shewed us light;
bind the sacrifice with cords,
yea even unto the horns of the altar.

O by Thy resurrection raise us up
unto newness of life,
supplying to us frames of repentance.
The God of peace,
who did bring again from the dead
the great Shepherd of the sheep,
through the blood of the everlasting covenant,
our Lord Jesus Christ,
perfect us in every good work,
to do His will,
working in us what is acceptable before Him,
through Jesus Christ,
to whom be glory for ever.

Thou who didst send down on Thy disciples
on this day
Thy Thrice-Holy Spirit,
withdraw not Thou the gift, O Lord, from us,
but renew it in us, day by day,
who ask Thee for it.

1. Confession

Merciful and pitiful Lord,
Long-suffering and full of pity,
I have sinned, Lord, I have sinned against Thee;
O me, wretched that I am,
I have sinned, Lord, against Thee
much and grievously,
in attending on vanities and lies.
I conceal nothing:
I make no excuses.
I give Thee glory, O Lord, this day,
I denounce against myself my sins;
Truly I have sinned before the Lord,
and thus and thus have I done.
I have sinned and perverted
that which was right,
and it profited me not.
And what shall I now say?
or with what shall I open my mouth?
What shall I answer, seeing I have done it?
Without plea, without defence, self-condemned, am I.
I have destroyed myself.
Unto Thee, O Lord, belongeth righteousness,
but unto me confusion of face,
because Thou art just in all that is come upon me;

for Thou hast done right,
but I have done wickedly.
And now, Lord, what is my hope?
Truly my hope is even in Thee,
if hope of salvation remain to me,
if Thy loving-kindness cover
the multitude of my iniquities.
O remember, what my substance is,
the work of Thine hands,
the likeness of Thy countenance,
the cost of Thy blood,
a name from Thy Name,
a sheep of Thy pasture,
a son of the covenant.
Despise not Thou the work of Thine own hands.
Hast Thou made for nought
Thine own image and likeness?
for nought, if Thou destroy it.
And what profit is there in my blood ?
Thine enemies will rejoice;
May they never rejoice, O Lord!
Grant not to them my destruction.
Look upon the face of Thine Anointed,
and in the Blood of Thy covenant,
the propitiation for the sins of the whole world,

Lord, be propitious unto me, a sinner ;
even unto me, O Lord, of sinners
chief, chiefest and greatest ;
For Thy Name's sake be merciful unto my sin,
for it is great: it exceeds.
For Thy Name's sake, that Name,
beside which, none other under heaven
is given among men,
whereby we must be saved,
the Spirit Himself helping our infirmities,
and making intercession for us,
with plaints unutterable.
For the tender yearnings of the Father,
the bloody wounds of the Son,
the unutterable plaints of the Spirit,
give ear, O Lord, have mercy, O Lord,
O Lord, hearken and do ;
defer not, for Thine own sake,
O my God.
For me, I forget not my sins,
they are ever before me ;
I remember them in the bitterness of my soul ;
I am anxious about them ;
I turn away and groan,
I have indignation and revenge

and wrath against myself.
I despise and bruise my own self,
that my penitence, Lord, O Lord,
is not deeper, is not fuller ;
help Thou mine impenitence.
And more, and still more,
pierce Thou, rend, crush my heart ;
and remit, forgive, pardon
what things are grief to me,
and offence of heart.
Cleanse Thou me from secret faults,
and keep Thy servant also from presumptuous sins.
Magnify Thy mercies towards the wretched sinner ;
and in season, Lord, say to me,
Be of good cheer ; thy sins are forgiven thee ;
My grace is sufficient for thee.
Say unto my soul, I am thy salvation.
Why art thou so heavy, O my soul ?
and why art thou so disquieted within thee ?
Return unto thy rest, O my soul,
for the Lord hath rewarded thee.
O Lord, rebuke me not in Thine indignation,
neither chasten me in Thy displeasure.
I said, I will confess my sins unto the Lord,
and so Thou forgavest the wickedness of my sin.

Lord, Thou knowest all my desire,
and my groaning is not hid from Thee.
Have mercy upon me, O God,
after Thy great goodness,
according to the multitude of Thy mercies
do away mine offences.
Thou shalt arise, and have mercy on me, O Lord,
for it is time that Thou have mercy upon me,
yea, the time is come.
If Thou, O Lord, shouldest mark iniquities,
O Lord, who shall stand ?
Enter not into judgment with Thy servant, O Lord,
for in Thy sight shall no man living be justified.

2. Prayer for Grace

My hands will I lift up
unto Thy commandments which I have loved.
Open Thou mine eyes that I may see,
incline my heart that I may desire,
order my steps that I may follow,
the way of Thy commandments.
O Lord God, be Thou to me a God,
and beside Thee none else,
none else, nought else with Thee.

Vouchsafe to me, to worship Thee and serve Thee
1. in truth of spirit,
2. in reverence of body,
3. in blessing of lips
4. in private and in public;
5. to pay honour to them that have the rule over me,
by obedience and submission,
to shew affection to my own,
by carefulness and providence;
6. to overcome evil with good ;
7. to possess my vessel in sanctification and honour;
8. to have my converse without covetousness,
content with what I have;
9. to speak the truth in love;
10. to be desirous not to lust,
not to lust passionately,
not to go after lusts.

(The Hedge of the Law, i. e. Precautions)

1. To bruise the serpent's head. *Gen*. iii. 15.
2. To remember my latter end. *Deut*. xxvii. 29.
3. To cut off opportunities. 2 *Cor*. xi. 12.
4. To be sober. 1 *Pet*. v. 8.
5. Not to sit idle. *Matt*. xx. 6.

6. To shun the wicked.   *Ps.* xxvi. 5.
7. To cleave to the good.   *Rom.* xii. 9.
8. To make a covenant with the eyes.   *Job* xxxi. 1.
9. To bring my body into subjection.   1 *Cor.* ix. 27.
10. To give myself unto prayer.   1 *Cor.* vii. 5.
11. To betake myself to penitence.   2 *Pet.* iii. 9.

Hedge up my way with thorns,
that I find not the path
for following vanity.
Hold Thou me in with bit and bridle,
lest I fall from Thee.
O Lord compel me to come in to Thee.

3. Profession

I believe, O Lord ,
in Thee, Father, Word, Spirit, One God
that by Thy fatherly love and power
all things were created ;—
that by Thy goodness and love to man
all things have been begun anew
in Thy Word,—
Who for us men and for our salvation,
was made flesh,
was conceived and born,

suffered and was crucified,
died and was buried,
descended and rose again,
ascended and sat down,
will return and will repay;—
that by the shining-forth and working
of Thy Holy Spirit,
hath been called out of the whole world
a peculiar people into a polity,
in belief of the truth
and sanctity of living:—
that in it we are partakers
of the communion of saints
and forgiveness of sins
in this world,—
that in it we are waiting
for resurrection of the flesh
and life everlasting
in the world to come.—
This most holy faith
which was once delivered to the saints
I believe, O Lord ;
help Thou mine unbelief,
and vouchsafe to me
to love the Father for His fatherly love,

to reverence the Almighty for His power,
as a faithful Creator, to commit my soul to Him
in well doing;
vouchsafe to me to partake
from Jesus of salvation,
from Christ of anointing,
from the Only-begotten of adoption;
to worship the Lord
for His conception in faith,
for His birth in humility,
for His sufferings in patience and hatred of sin;
for His cross to crucify beginnings,
for His death to mortify the flesh,
for His burial to bury evil thoughts in good works,
for His descent to meditate upon hell,
for His resurrection upon newness of life,
for His ascension, to mind things above,
for His sitting on high, to mind the good things on
His right,
for His return, to fear His second appearance,
for judgment, to judge myself ere I be judged.
From the Spirit
vouchsafe me the breath of salutary grace.
In the Holy Catholic Church
to have my own calling, and holiness, and portion,

and a fellowship
of her sacred rites, and prayers,
fastings and groans,
vigils, tears, and sufferings,
for assurance of remission of sins,
for hope of resurrection and translation
to eternal life.

4. Intercession

O Hope of all the ends of the earth,
and of them that remain in the broad sea;
O Thou on whom our fathers hoped,
and Thou didst deliver them;
on whom they waited,
and were not confounded;
O my Hope from my youth,
from my mother's breasts;
on whom I have been cast from the womb,
be Thou my hope
now and evermore,
and my portion in the land of the living:
In Thy nature,
in Thy names, in Thy types,
in word and in deed,

My Hope,
let me not be disappointed of my hope.
O the Hope of all the ends of the earth,
remember Thy whole creation for good,
visit the world in Thy compassion ;
O guardian of men,
O loving Lord,
remember all our race.
Thou who hast shut up all in unbelief,
on all have pity, O Lord.
O Thou who didst die and rise again,
to be Lord both of the dead and living,
live we or die we,
Thou art our Lord ;
Lord, have pity on living and dead.
O helper of the helpless,
seasonable aid in affliction,
remember all who are in necessity,
and need Thy succour.
O God of grace and truth,
establish all who stand in truth and grace,
restore all who are sick with heresies and sins.
O wholesome defence of Thine anointed,
remember Thy congregation
which Thou hast purchased and redeemed of old.

O grant to all believers
one heart and one soul.
Thou that walkest amid the golden candlesticks,
remove not our candlestick
out of its place.
Amend what are wanting,
establish what remain,
which Thou art ready to cast away,
which are ready to die.
O Lord of the harvest
send forth labourers, made sufficient by Thee,
into Thy harvest.
O portion of those
who wait in Thy temple,
grant to our clergy,
rightly to divide the word of truth
rightly to walk in it ;
grant to Thy Christian people
to obey and submit to them.
O King of nations, unto the ends
of the earth ;
strengthen all the states
of the inhabited world,
as being Thy ordinance,
though a creation of man.

Scatter the nations that delight in war,
make wars to cease in all the earth.
O expectation of the isles and their hope,
Lord, save this island,
and all the country in which we sojourn,
from all affliction, peril, and need.
Lord of lords, Ruler of rulers,
remember all rulers
to whom Thou hast given rule in the earth,
and O remember specially
our divinely-guarded king,
and work with him more and more,
and prosper his way in all things.
Speak good things unto his heart,
for Thy Church, and all Thy people,
grant to him profound and perpetual peace,
that in his tranquillity
we may lead a quiet and peaceable life
in all godliness and honesty.
O Thou by whom are ordained the powers that be,
grant to those who are chief in court,
to be chief in virtue and Thy fear ;
grant to the Parliament Thy holy wisdom ;
to our great men, to do nothing against
but for the truth ;

to the courts of law, Thy judgments,
to judge in all things concerning all
without preference, without partiality.
O God of armies,
give a prosperous course and strength
to all the Christian army,
against the enemies of our most holy faith.
Grant to our population
to be subject unto the higher powers,
not only for wrath, but also for conscience-sake.
Grant to farmers and graziers good seasons ;
to the fleet and fishers fair weather ;
to tradesmen, not to overreach one another ;
to mechanics, to pursue their business lawfully,
down to the meanest workman,
down to the poor.
O God, not of us only but of our seed,
bless our children among us,
to advance in wisdom as in stature,
and in favour with Thee and with men.
Thou who wouldest have us provide for our own,
and hatest the unnatural,
remember, Lord, my relations according to the flesh ;
grant me to speak peace concerning them,
and to seek their good.

Thou who willest us to make return
to our benefactors,
remember, Lord, for good,
all from whom I have received good ;
keep them alive that they may be blessed upon earth,
and deliver them not
into the will of their enemies.
Thou who hast noted
the man who neglects his own, as worse
than an infidel,
remember in Thy good pleasure
all those in my household.
Peace be to my house,
the Son of peace upon all in it.
Thou who wouldest that our righteousness exceed
the righteousness of sinners,
grant me, Lord, to love those who love me ;
my own friend, and my father's friend,
and my friend's children,
never to forsake.
Thou who wouldest that we overcome
evil with good,
and pray for those who persecute us,
have pity on mine enemies, Lord,
as on myself ;

and lead them together with me
to Thy heavenly kingdom.
Thou who grantest the prayers of thy servants
one for another,
remember, Lord, for good,
and pity all those
who remember me in their prayers,
or whom I have promised to remember in mine.
Thou who acceptest diligence in every good work,
remember, Lord, as if they prayed to Thee,
those who for any good reason
give not time to prayer.
Arise, and have mercy
on those who are in the last necessity,
for it is time that Thou hast mercy upon them,
yea the time is come.
Have mercy on them, O Lord,
as on me also, when in extremities.
Remember, Lord,
infants, children, the grown, the young,
the middle aged, the old,
hungry, thirsty, naked, sick,
prisoners, foreigners, friendless, unburied,
all in extreme age and weakness,
possessed with devils, and tempted to suicide,

troubled by unclean spirits,
the hopeless, the sick in soul or body, the weak-hearted,
all in prison and chains, all under sentence of death ;
orphans, widows, foreigners, travellers, voyagers,
women with child, women who give suck,
all in bitter servitude, or mines, or galleys,
or in loneliness.
Thou, Lord, shalt save both man and beast,
how excellent is Thy mercy, O God !
And the children of men shall put their trust
under the shadow of Thy wings.
The Lord bless us, and keep us,
and shew the light of His countenance upon us,
And be merciful unto us,
The Lord lift up His countenance upon us,
And give us peace !
I commend to Thee, O Lord,
my soul, and my body,
my mind, and my thoughts,
my prayers, and my vows,
my senses, and my limbs,
my words, and my works [a],
my life, and my death ;
my brothers, and my sisters,

[a] Page 172, Edit. 1675.

and their children ;
my friends, my benefactors, my well wishers,
those who have a claim on me ;
my kindred, and my neighbours,
my country, and all Christendom.
I commend to Thee, Lord,
my impulses, and my startings,
my intentions, and my attempts,
my going out, and my coming in,
my sitting down, and my rising up.

5. Praise

Up with our hearts ;
we lift them to the Lord.
O how very meet, and right, and fitting, and due,
in all, and for all,
at all times, places, manners,
in every season, every spot,
everywhere, always, altogether,
to remember Thee, to worship Thee,
to confess to Thee, to praise Thee,
to bless Thee, to hymn Thee,
to give thanks to Thee,
Maker, nourisher, guardian, governor,
preserver, worker, perfecter of all,

Lord and Father,
King and God,
fountain of life and immortality,
treasure of everlasting goods.
Whom the heavens hymn,
and the heaven of heavens,
the Angels and all the heavenly powers,
one to other crying continually,—
and we the while, weak and unworthy,
under their feet,—
Holy, Holy, Holy
Lord the God of Hosts ;
full is the whole heaven,
and the whole earth,
of the majesty of Thy glory.
Blessed be the glory of the Lord
out of His place,
For His Godhead, His mysteriousness,
His height, His sovereignty, His almightiness,
His eternity, His providence.
The Lord is my strength, my stony rock, and my defence,
my deliverer, my succour, my buckler,
the horn also of my salvation and my refuge.

The Second Day

Introduction

My voice shalt Thou hear betimes, O Lord,
early in the morning
will I direct my prayer unto Thee,
and will look up.
Blessed art Thou, O Lord,
who didst create the firmament of heaven,
the heavens and the heaven of heavens,
the heavenly powers,
Angels, Archangels,
Cherubim, Seraphim,
waters above the heavens,
mists and exhalations,
for showers, dew, hail, snow as wool,
hoar frost as ashes, ice as morsels,
clouds from the ends of the earth,
lightnings, thunders, winds out of Thy treasures,
storms ;
waters beneath the heavens,
for drinking and for bathing.

1. Confession

I will confess my sins,
and the sins of my fathers,
for I have transgressed and neglected Thee, O Lord,
and walked perversely before Thee.
Set not, O Lord, set not my misdeeds before Thee,
nor my life in the light of Thy countenance,
But pardon the iniquity of Thy servant,
according to Thy great mercy ;
as Thou hast been merciful to him from a child,
even so now.
I have sinned, what shall I do unto Thee,
O Thou preserver of men ?
Why hast Thou set me as a mark against Thee,
so that I am a burden to myself ?
O pardon my transgression,
and take away mine iniquity.
Deliver me from going down to the pit,
for Thou hast found a ransom.
Have mercy on me, Son of David,
Lord, help me.
Yea, Lord, even the dogs eat of the crumbs
which fall from their masters' table.
Have patience with me, Lord,

yet I have not wherewith to pay,

I confess to Thee ;

forgive me the whole debt, I beseech Thee.

How long wilt Thou forget me, O Lord ? for ever ?

How long wilt Thou hide Thy face from me ?

How long shall I seek counsel in my soul,

and be vexed in my heart day and night ?

How long shall mine enemies triumph over me ?

Consider and hear me, O Lord my God,

lighten mine eyes that I sleep not in death,

lest mine enemy say I have prevailed against him,

for if I be cast down, they that trouble me will

rejoice at it ;

but my trust is in Thy mercy.

2. Prayer for Grace

Remove from me

(The Ten Commandments.)

1. all iniquity and profaneness, super-stition, and hypocrisy.
2. worship of idols, of persons.
3. rash oath, and curse.
4. neglect or indecency of worship.
5. haughtiness and recklessness.
6. strife and wrath.
7. passion and corruption.

8. indolence and fraud.

9. lying and injuriousness.

10. every evil notion, every impure thought, every base desire, every unseemly thought.

Grant to me,

1. to be religious and pious.

2. to worship and swear.

3. to bless and serve truly.

4. to confess meetly in the congregation.

5. affection and obedience.

6. patience and good temper.

7. purity and soberness.

8. contentedness and goodness.

9. truth and incorruptness.

10. good thoughts, perseverance to the end.

3. Profession

I believe in God,

1. the Father, Almighty, Maker of heaven and earth.

2. And in Jesus Christ, His Only-begotten Son, our Lord.

(1.) conceived of the Holy Ghost,

(2.) born of Mary, ever-virgin,

(3.) suffered under Pontius Pilate,
(4.) crucified,
(5.) dead,
(6.) buried.—
(1.) descended into hell,
(2.) risen from the dead,
(3.) ascended into heaven,
(4.) set down on the right hand,
(5.) to return thence,
(6.) to judge both quick and dead.

3. And in the Holy Ghost,

(1.) The Holy Church,
(2.) Catholic,
(3.) communion of saints,
(4.) remission of sins,
(5.) resurrection of flesh,
(6.) life everlasting.

And now, Lord, what is my hope?
  Truly my hope is even in Thee;
  in Thee, O Lord, have I trusted,
    let me never be confounded.

4. Intercession

Let us pray God,
for the whole creation ;
for the supply of seasons,
healthy, fruitful, peaceful ;
for the whole race of mankind ;
for those who are not Christians ;
for the conversion of Atheists, the ungodly ;
Gentiles, Turks, and Jews ;
for all Christians ;
for restoration of all
who languish in errors and sins ;
for confirmation of all
who have been granted truth and grace ;
for succour and comfort of all
who are dispirited, infirm, distressed, unsettled,
men and women ;
for thankfulness and sobriety in all
who are hearty, healthy, prosperous, quiet,
men and women ;
For the Catholic Church,
its establishment and increase ;
for the Eastern,
its deliverance and union ;

for the Western,
    its adjustment and peace ;
for the British,
    the supply of what is wanting in it,
    the strengthening of what remains in it ;
for the episcopate, presbytery, Christian people ;
    for the states of the inhabited world ;
        for Christian states,
        far off, near at hand ;
          for our own ;
          for all in rule ;
      for our divinely-guarded king,
      the queen and the prince ;
for those who have place in the court ;
    for parliament and judicature,
      army and police,
    commons and their leaders,
farmers, graziers, fishers, merchants,
      traders, and mechanics,
down to mean workmen, and the poor ;
    for the rising generation ;
for the good nurture of all the royal family,
    of the young ones of the nobility ;
for all in universities, in inns of court,
    in schools in town or country,

in apprenticeships ;

for those who have a claim on me from relationship,

for brothers and sisters,

that God's blessing may be on them,

and on their children ;

or from benefits conferred,

that Thy recompence may be on all

who have benefited me,

who have ministered to me in carnal things ;

or from trust placed in me,

for all whom I have educated,

all whom I have ordained :

for my college, my parish,

Southwell, St. Paul's, Westminster,

Dioceses of Chichester, Ely, and my present,

clergy, people, helps, governments,

the deanery in the chapel royal,

the almonry,

the colleges committed to me [a] ;

or from natural kindness,

for all who love me,

though I know them not ;

or from Christian love ;

for those who hate me without cause,

[a] As Visitor.

some too, even on account of truth and righteousness ;
or from neighbourhood,
for all who dwell near me
peaceably and harmlessly ;
or from promise,
for all whom I have promised to remember
in my prayers ;
or from mutual offices,
for all who remember me in their prayers,
and ask of me the same ;
or from stress of engagements,
for all who on sufficient reasons fail to call
upon Thee ;
for all who have no intercessor
in their own behalf ;
for all who at present are in agony
of extreme necessity or deep affliction ;
for all who are attempting any good work
which will bring glory to the Name of God
or some great good to the Church ;
for all who act nobly
either towards things sacred or towards the poor ;
for all who have ever been offended by me
either in word or in deed.
God have mercy on me and bless me ;

God shew the light of His countenance upon me
and pity me.
God bless me, even our God,
God bless me and receive my prayer ;
O direct my life towards Thy commandments,
hallow my soul,
purify my body,
correct my thoughts,
cleanse my desires,
soul and body, mind and spirit,
heart and reins.
Renew me thoroughly, O God,
for, if Thou wilt, Thou canst.

5. Praise

The Lord, the Lord God,
merciful and pitiful,
long-suffering and full of pity, and true,
keeping pity for thousands,
taking away iniquities and unrighteousnesses and sins;
not clearing the guilty one,
bringing sins of fathers upon children.
I will bless the Lord at all times,
His praise shall ever be in my mouth.

Glory to God in the highest,
and on earth peace,
goodwill towards men.

The Angels,	guardianship ;
Archangels,	glory ;
Powers,	marvels ;
Thrones,	judgment ;
Dominions,	beneficence ;
Principalities,	government ;
Authorities,	against devils ;
Cherubim,	knowledge ;
Seraphim,	love.

The Third Day

Introduction

O God, Thou art my God,
early will I seek Thee.
Blessed art Thou, O Lord,
who gatheredst the water into the sea,
and broughtest to sight the earth,
and madest to sprout
herb and fruit-tree.
There are the depths and the sea as on an heap,
lakes, rivers, springs ;
earth, continent, and isles,
mountains, hills, and valleys ;
glebe, meadows, glades,
green pasture, corn, and hay ;
herbs and flowers
for food, enjoyment, medicine ;
fruit-trees bearing
wine, oil, and spices,

and trees for wood ;
and things beneath the earth,
stones, metals, minerals, coal,
blood and fire, and vapour of smoke.

1. Confession

Who can understand his errors ?
Cleanse Thou me from secret faults.
Keep back Thy servant also from presumptuous sins,
lest they have the dominion over me.
For Thy Name's sake,
be merciful unto my sin,
for it is great.
My iniquities have taken such hold upon me
that I am not able to look up,
yea, they are more in number than the hairs of my
head,
and my heart hath failed me.
Be pleased, O Lord, to deliver me,
Make haste, O Lord, to help me.
Magnify Thy mercies upon me,
O Thou who savest them that trust in Thee.
I said, Lord, have mercy upon me,
heal my soul, for I have sinned against Thee ;
I have sinned, but I am confounded,

and I turn from my evil ways,
and I turn unto mine own heart,
and with my whole heart I turn unto Thee ;
and I seek Thy face,
and I beseech Thee, saying,
I have sinned, I have committed iniquity,
I have done unjustly.
I know, O Lord, the plague of my heart,
and lo, I turn to Thee with all my heart,
and with all my strength.
And Thou, O Lord, now from Thy dwelling-place,
and from the glorious throne of Thy kingdom
in heaven,
O hear the prayer
and the supplication of Thy servant ;
and be propitious towards Thy servant
and heal his soul.
O God, be merciful to me a sinner,
be merciful to me the chief of sinners.
Father, I have sinned against heaven, and before Thee,
and am no more worthy to be called Thy son,
make me one of Thy hired servants ;
Make me one, or even the last,
or the least among all.
What profit is there in my blood,

when I go down to the pit ?
shall the dust give thanks unto Thee ?
or shall it declare Thy truth ?
Hear, O Lord, and have mercy upon me ;
Lord, be Thou my helper ;
Turn my heaviness into joy,
my dreamings into earnestness,
my falls into clearings of myself,
my guilt, my offence into indignation,
my sin into fear,
my transgression into vehement desire,
my unrighteousness into strictness,
my pollution into revenge.

2. Prayer for Grace

Hosanna in the highest[a].
Remember me, O Lord,
with the favour that Thou bearest unto Thy people,
O visit me with Thy salvation ;
that I may see the felicity of Thy chosen,
and rejoice in the gladness of Thy people,
and give thanks with Thine inheritance.
There is glory which shall be revealed ;
for when the Judge cometh

[a] Vide p. 186, edit. 1675.

some shall see Thy face cheerful,
and shall be placed on the right,
and shall hear those most welcome words,
"Come, ye blessed."
They shall be caught up in clouds
to meet the Lord ;
they shall enter into gladness,
they shall enjoy the sight of Him,
they shall be ever with Him.
These alone, only these are blessed
among the sons of men.
O to me the meanest grant the meanest place,
there under their feet ;
under the feet of Thine elect,
the meanest among them.
And that this may be,
let me find grace in Thy sight
to have grace,   (*Heb.* xii. 28.)
so as to serve Thee acceptably
with reverence and godly fear.
Let me find that second grace,
not to receive in vain   (2 *Cor.* vi. 1.)
the first grace,
not to come short of it ; (*Heb.* xii. 15.)
yea, not to neglect it, (1 *Tim.* iv. 14.)

so as to fall from it,   (*Gal.* v. 4.)
but to stir it up,   (2 *Tim.* i. 6.)
so as to increase in it, (2 *Pet.* iii. 18.)
yea, to abide in it
till the end of my life.
And O, perfect for me what is lacking
of Thy gifts,
of faith,   help Thou mine unbelief,
of hope,   establish my trembling hope,
of love,   kindle its smoking flax.
Shed abroad Thy love in my heart,
so that I may love Thee,
my friend in Thee, my enemy for Thee.
O Thou who givest grace to the humble-minded,
also give me grace to be humble-minded.
O Thou who never failest those who fear Thee,
my Fear and my Hope,
let me fear one thing only,
the fearing ought more than Thee.
As I would that men should do to me
so may I do to them ;
not to have thoughts beyond what I should think,
but to have thoughts unto sobriety.
Shine on those who sit in darkness,
and the shadow of death ;

guide our feet into the way of peace,
that we may have the same thoughts
one with another,
rightly to divide, rightly to walk,
to edify,
with one accord, with one mouth
to glorify God ;
and if ought otherwise,
to walk in the same rule
as far as we have attained ;
to maintain order,
decency and stedfastness.

3. Profession

Godhead, paternal love, power,
providence :
salvation, anointing, adoption,
lordship ;
conception, birth, passion,
cross, death, burial,
descent, resurrection, ascent,
sitting, return, judgment ;
Breath and Holiness,
calling from the Universal,
hallowing in the Universal,

communion of saints, and of saintly things,
resurrection,
life eternal.

4. Intercession

Hosanna on the earth [b].
Remember, O Lord,
to crown the year with Thy goodness ;
for the eyes of all look towards Thee,
and Thou givest their food in due season.
Thou openest Thine hand,
and fillest all things living with plenteousness.
And on us, O Lord, vouchsafe
the blessings of heaven and the dew above,
blessings of fountains and the deep beneath,
courses of sun, conjunctions of moons,
summits of eastern mountains, of the everlasting hills,
fulness of the earth and of produce thereof,
good seasons, wholesome weather,
full crops, plenteous fruits,
health of body, peaceful times,
mild government, kind laws,

[b] Continuation of the supplication broken by "*Profession.*"
Vide p. 192, edit. 1675.

wise councils, equal judgments,
loyal obedience, vigorous justice,
fertility in resources, fruitfulness in begetting,
ease in bearing, happiness in offspring,
careful nurture, sound training,
That our sons may grow up as the young plants,
our daughters as the polished corners of the temple,
that our garners may be full and plenteous
with all manner of store,
that our sheep may bring forth thousands
and ten thousands in our streets :
that there be no decay,
no leading into captivity
and no complaining in our streets.

5. Praise

ᶜThou, O Lord, art praised in Sion,
and unto Thee shall the vow be performed
in Jerusalem.
Thou art worthy, O Lord our God,
the Holy One,
to receive glory, and honour, and power.
Thou that hearest the prayer,

ᶜ Vide p. 172, edit. 1675.

unto Thee shall all flesh come,
my flesh shall come.
My misdeeds prevail against me,
O be Thou merciful unto our sins ;
that I may come and give thanks
with all Thy works,
and bless Thee with Thy holy ones.
O Lord, open Thou my lips,
and my mouth shall shew forth Thy praise.
My soul doth praise the Lord,
for the goodness He hath done
to the whole creation,
and to the whole race of men ;
for Thy mercies towards myself,
soul, body, and estate,
gifts of grace, nature, and fortune ;
for all benefits received,
for all successes, now or heretofore,
for any good thing done ;
for health, credit, competency,
safety, gentle estate, quiet.
Thou hast not cut off as a weaver my life,
nor from day even to night made an end of me.
He hath vouchsafed me life and breath
until this hour,

from childhood, youth, and hitherto
even unto age.
He holdeth our soul in life
and suffereth not our feet to slip ;
rescuing me from perils, sicknesses,
poverty, bondage,
public shame, evil chances ;
keeping me from perishing in my sins,
fully waiting my conversion,
leaving in me return into my heart,
remembrance of my latter end,
shame, horror, grief,
for my past sins ;
fuller and larger, larger and fuller,
more and still more, O my Lord,
storing me with good hope
of their remission,
through repentance and its works,
in the power of the thrice-holy Keys,
and the mysteries in Thy Church.
Wherefore day by day
for these Thy benefits towards me,
which I remember,—
wherefore also for others very many
which I have let slip

from their number, from my forgetfulness,—
for those which I wished, knew and asked,
and those I asked not, knew not, wished not,—
I confess and give thanks to Thee,
I bless and praise Thee, as is fit, and every day,
And I pray with my whole soul,
and with my whole mind I pray.
Glory be to Thee, O Lord, glory to Thee ;
glory to Thee, and glory to Thine All-holy Name,
for all Thy Divine perfections in them ;
for Thine incomprehensible and
unimaginable goodness,
and Thy pity towards sinners
and unworthy men,
and towards me of all sinners
far the most unworthy.
Yea, O Lord,
for this, and for the rest,
Glory to Thee,
and praise, and blessing, and thanksgiving,
with the voices and concert of voices
of Angels and of men,
of all Thy saints in heaven,
and all Thy creatures in heaven or earth,
and of me, beneath their feet,

unworthy and wretched sinner,
Thy abject creature,
now, in this day and hour,
and every day till **my** last breath,
and till the end **of** the world,
and for ages upon ages.

The Fourth Day

Introduction

I have thought upon Thee, O Lord,
when I was waking,
for Thou hast been my helper.
Blessed art Thou, O Lord,
who madest the two Lights, Sun and Moon,
greater and lesser,
and the stars
for light, for signs, for seasons,
spring, summer, autumn, winter,
days, weeks, months, years,
to rule over day and night.

1. Confession

Behold, Thou art angry, for we have sinned.
We are all as an unclean thing,
and all our righteousnesses
as filthy rags.

We all do fade as a leaf,
and our iniquities, like the wind,
have taken us away.
But now, O Lord, Thou art our Father,
we are clay, all Thy handiwork.
Be not wroth very sore,
nor remember iniquity for ever,
behold, see, we beseech Thee,
we are all Thy people.
O Lord, though our iniquities testify against us,
do Thou it for Thy Name's sake ;
for our backslidings are many,
we have sinned against Thee.
Yet Thou, O Lord, art in the midst of us,
and we are called by Thy Name,
leave us not.
O Hope of Israel,
The Saviour thereof in time of trouble,
why shouldest Thou be as a stranger in the land,
and as a wayfaring man that turneth aside
to tarry for a night ?
why shouldest Thou be as a man astonished,
as a mighty man that cannot save ?
Be merciful to our unrighteousnesses,
and our iniquities remember no more.

Lord, I am carnal,
　　sold under sin ;
there dwelleth in me, that is, in my flesh,
　　no good thing ;
for the good that I would, I do not,
but the evil which I would not, that I do.
I consent unto the law that it is good,
　　I delight in it after the inner man ;
But I see another law in my members,
　　warring against the law of my mind,
　　and enslaving me to the law of sin.
　　Wretched man that I am,
who shall deliver me from the body of this death ?
　　I thank God through Jesus Christ,
　　that where sin abounded,
　　grace hath much more abounded.
O Lord, Thy goodness leadeth me to repentance :
　　O give me sometime repentance
to recover me from the snare of the devil,
　　who am taken captive by him
　　at his will.
Sufficient for me the past time of my life
　　to have done the will of lusts,
walking in lasciviousness, revelling, drunkenness,
　　and in other excess of profligacy.

O Lamb without blemish and without spot,
who hast redeemed me with Thy precious Blood,
in that very Blood pity me and save me ;
in that Blood,
and in that very Name,
besides which is none other under heaven
given among men,
by which we must be saved.
O God, Thou knowest my foolishness,
and my sins are not hid from Thee.
Lord, Thou knowest all my desire,
and my groaning is not hid from Thee.
Let not them that trust in Thee,
O Lord God of hosts,
be ashamed for my cause ;
let not those that seek Thee be confounded
through me,
O Lord God of Israel.
Take me out of the mire that I sink not ;
O let me be delivered from them that hate me
and out of the deep waters ;
Let not the water flood drown me,
neither let the deep swallow me up,
and let not the pit shut her mouth upon me.

2. Prayer for Grace

[Defend me from]

	Pride	Amorite.
(against seven deadly sins.)	envy	Hittite.
	wrath	Perizzite.
	gluttony	Girgashite.
	lechery	Hivite.
(covetousness.)	the cares of life . . .	Canaanite.
(sloth.)	lukewarm indifference .	Jebusite.

[Give me]

Humility, pitifulness, patience,
sobriety, purity, contentment, ready zeal.
One thing have I desired of the Lord
which I will require[a],
that I may dwell in the house of the Lord
all the days of my life,
to behold the fair beauty of the Lord,
and to visit His temple.
Two things have I required of Thee, O Lord,
deny Thou me not before I die ;
remove far from me vanity and lies ;
give me neither poverty nor riches,
feed me with food convenient for me ;
lest I be full and deny Thee

[a] Vide p. 194, edit. 1675.

and say, who is the Lord ?
or lest I be poor and steal,
and take the Name of my God in vain.
Let me learn to abound,
let me learn to suffer need,
in whatsoever state I am,
therewith to be content.
For nothing earthly, temporal, mortal,
to long nor to wait.
Grant me a happy life
in piety, gravity, purity,
in all things good and fair,
in cheerfulness, in health, in credit,
in competency, in safety, in gentle estate, in quiet ;
a happy death,
a deathless happiness.

3. Profession

I believe
in the Father, benevolent affection ;
in the Almighty, saving power ;
in the Creator, providence
for guarding, ruling, perfecting the universe.
In Jesus, salvation,
in Christ, anointing ;

in the Only-begotten Son, sonship,
in the Lord, a master's treatment,
in His conception and birth
the cleansing of our unclean conception and birth ;
in His sufferings, which we owed,
that we might not pay ;
in His cross the curse of the law removed ;
in His death the sting of death ;
in His burial eternal destruction in the tomb ;
in His descent, whither we ought,
that we might not go ;
in His resurrection,
as the first fruits of them that sleep ;
in His ascent, to prepare a place for us ;
in His sitting, to appear and intercede ;
in His return, to take unto Him His own ;
in His judgment, to render to each
according to his works.
In the Holy Ghost, power from on high,
transforming unto sanctity
from without and invisibly,
yet inwardly and evidently.
In the Church, a body mystical
of the called out of the whole world,
unto intercourse in faith and holiness.

In the communion of Saints, members of this body,
a mutual participation in holy things,
for confidence of remission of sins,
for hope of resurrection, of translation,
to life everlasting.

4. Intercession

And I have hoped in Thy mercy
from everlasting to everlasting.
How excellent is Thy mercy, O Lord ;
If I have hope, it is in Thy mercy,
O let me not be disappointed of my hope.
Moreover we beseech Thee,
remember all, Lord, for good ;
have pity upon all, O Sovereign Lord,
be reconciled with us all.
Give peace to the multitudes of Thy people ;
scatter offences ;
abolish wars ;
stop the uprisings of heresies.
Thy peace and love
vouchsafe to us, O God our Saviour,
the Hope of all the ends of the earth.

Remember to crown the year
with Thy goodness ;
for the eyes of all wait upon Thee,
and Thou givest them their meat in due season.
Thou openest Thy hand,
and fillest all things living with plenteousness.
Remember Thy Holy Church,
from one end of the earth to the other ;
and give her peace,
whom Thou hast redeemed with Thy precious blood ;
and establish her
unto the end of the world.
Remember those who bear fruit, and act nobly,
in Thy holy Churches,
and who remember the poor and needy ;
recompense to them
Thy rich and heavenly gifts ;
vouchsafe to them,
for things earthly, heavenly,
for corruptible, incorruptible,
for temporal, eternal.
Remember those who are in virginity,
and purity and ascetic life ;
also those who live in honourable marriage,
in Thy reverence and fear.

Remember every Christian soul
in affliction, distress, and trial,
and in need of Thy pity and succour ;
also our brethren in captivity, prison, chains,
and bitter bondage ;
supplying return to the wandering,
health to the sick,
deliverance to the captives.
Remember religious and faithful kings,
whom Thou hast given to rule
upon the earth ;
and especially remember, Lord,
our divinely-guarded king ;
strengthen his kingdom,
subdue to him all adversaries,
speak good things to his heart,
for Thy Church, and all Thy people.
Vouchsafe to him deep and undisturbed peace,
that in his serenity
we may lead a quiet and peaceable life
with all godliness and honesty.
Remember, Lord, all power
and authority,
our brethren in the court,
those who are chief in council and judgment,

and all by land and sea
waging Thy wars for us.
Moreover, Lord, remember graciously
our holy Fathers,
the honourable Presbytery, and all the Clergy,
rightly dividing the Word of Truth,
and rightly walking in it.
Remember, Lord, our brethren around us,
and praying with us in this holy hour,
for their zeal and earnestness-sake.
Remember also those who on fair reasons are away,
and pity them and us
in the multitude of Thy pity.
Fill our garners with all manner of store,
preserve our marriages in peace and concord,
nourish our infants,
lead forward our youth,
sustain our aged,
comfort the weak-hearted,
gather together the scattered,
restore the wanderers,
and knit them to Thy Holy Catholic Apostolic
Church.
Set free the troubled
with unclean spirits,

voyage with the voyagers,
travel with the travellers,
stand forth for the widow,
shield the orphan,
rescue the captive,
heal the sick.
Those who are on trial, in mines, in exile, in galleys,
in whatever affliction, necessity, and emergence,
remember, O God ;
and all who need Thy great mercy ;
and those who love us,
and those who hate ;
and those who have desired us unworthy
to make mention of them in our prayers ;
and all Thy people remember, O Lord, our God,
and upon all pour out Thy rich pity,
to all performing their requests for salvation ;
and those of whom we have not made mention,
through ignorance, forgetfulness, or number
of names,
do Thou Thyself remember, O God,
who knowest the stature and appellation of each,
who knowest every one from his mother's womb.
For Thou art, O Lord, the Succour of the succourless,
the Hope of the hopeless,

The Saviour of the tempest-tost,
the Harbour of the voyager,
the Physician of the sick,
do Thou Thyself become all things to all men.
O Thou who knowest each man and his petition,
each house, and its need,
deliver, O Lord, this city,
and all the country in which we sojourn,
from plague, famine, earthquake, flood,
fire, sword, hostile invasion,
and civil war.
End the schisms of the Churches,
quench the haughty cries of the nations,
and receive us all into Thy kingdom,
acknowledging us as sons of light ;
and Thy peace and love
vouchsafe to us, O Lord, our God.
Remember O Lord, our God,
all spirits and all flesh
which we have remembered, and which we have not.
And the close of our life,
Lord, Lord, direct in peace,
Christianly, acceptably, and, should it please Thee,
painlessly,
gathering us together under the feet of Thine elect,

when Thou wilt and how Thou wilt,
only without shame and sins.
The brightness of the Lord our God be upon us,
prosper Thou the work of our hands upon us,
O prosper Thou our handiwork.
Be, Lord,
within me to strengthen me,
without me to guard me,
over me to shelter me,
beneath me to stablish me,
before me to guide me,
after me to forward me,
round about me to secure me.

5. Praise

Blessed art Thou, Lord, God of Israel,
our Father,
from everlasting to everlasting.
Thine, O Lord,
is the greatness and the power,
the triumph and the victory,
the praise and the strength,
for Thou rulest over all
in heaven and on earth.

At Thy face every king is troubled,
and every nation.
Thine, O Lord, is the kingdom
and the supremacy over all,
and over all rule.
With Thee is wealth, and glory is from
Thy countenance ;
Thou rulest over all, O Lord,
the Ruler of all rule ;
and in Thine hand is strength and power,
and in Thine hand to give to all things
greatness and strength.
And now, Lord, we confess to Thee
and we praise Thy glorious Name.

The Fifth Day

Introduction

We are satisfied with Thy mercy, O Lord,
in the morning.
Blessed art Thou, O Lord,
who broughtest forth from the water
creeping things of life,
and whales,
and winged fowl.

Be Thou exalted, O God, above the heavens,
and Thy glory above all the earth.
By Thy Ascension, O Lord,
draw us too after Thee,
that we savour of what is above,
not of things on the earth.

By the marvellous mystery
of the Holy Body and precious Blood,
on the evening of this day,
Lord, have mercy.

1. Confession

Thou who hast said,
" As I live, saith the Lord,
I will not the death of a sinner,
but that the ungodly return from his way
and live ;
turn ye, turn ye from your wicked way,
for why will ye die, O house of Israel ? "
turn us, O Lord, to Thee,
and so shall we be turned.
Turn us from all our ungodlinesses,
and let them not be to us for punishments.
I have sinned, I have committed iniquity,
I have done wickedly,
from Thy precepts, and Thy judgments.
To Thee, O Lord, righteousness,
and to me confusion of face,
as at this day,
in our despicableness,
wherewith Thou hast despised us.
Lord, to us confusion of face,
and to our rulers
who have sinned against Thee.
Lord, in all things is Thy righteousness,

unto all Thy righteousness ;
let then Thine anger and Thy fury be turned away,
and cause Thy face to shine
upon Thy servant.
O my God, incline Thine ear and hear,
open Thine eyes and see my desolation.
O Lord hear, O Lord forgive,
O Lord hearken and do ;
defer not for Thine own sake, O my God,
for Thy servant is called by Thy Name.
In many things we offend all ;
Lord, let Thy mercy rejoice against Thy judgment
in my sins.
If I say I have no sin, I deceive myself,
and the truth is not in me ;
but I confess my sins many and grievous,
and Thou, O Lord, art faithful and just,
to forgive me my sins when I confess them.
Yea, for this too
I have an Advocate with Thee to Thee,
Thy Only-begotten Son, the Righteous.
May He be the propitiation for my sins,
who is also for the whole world.
Will the Lord cast off for ever ?
and will He be no more intreated ?

Is His mercy clean gone for ever ?
and is His promise come utterly to an end
for evermore ?
Hath God forgotten to be gracious ?
and will He shut up His loving kindness
in displeasure ?
And I said, It is mine own infirmity ;
but I will remember the years of the right hand
of the most Highest.

2. Prayer for Grace

[Give me grace]
to put aside every weight,
and the sin that doth so easily beset us ;
all filthiness
and superfluity of naughtiness,
lust of the flesh, of the eyes,
pride of life,
every motion of flesh and spirit
alienated from the will of Thy sanctity :
to be poor in spirit,
that I have a portion in the kingdom of heaven ;
to mourn, that I be comforted ;
to be meek, that I inherit the earth ;

to hunger and thirst for righteousness,
that I be filled ;
to be pitiful, that I be pitied ;
to be pure in heart, that I see God ;
to be a peace-maker, that I be called the son of God ;
to be prepared for persecutions and revilings
for righteousness' sake,
that my reward be in heaven,—
all this, grant to me, O Lord.

3. Profession

I, coming to God,
believe that He is,
and that He is a rewarder of them
that diligently seek Him.
I know that my Redeemer liveth,
that He is Christ, the Son of the Living God,
that He is truly the Saviour of the world,
that He came into the world to save sinners,
of whom I am chief.
Through the grace of Jesus Christ
we believe that we shall be saved
like as our fathers.
I know that my skin shall rise up upon the earth,
which undergoeth these things.

I believe to see the goodness of the Lord
in the land of the living.
Our heart shall rejoice in Him,
because we have hoped in His holy Name,
in the Name of the Father,
of the Saviour, Mediator, Intercessor, Redeemer,
of the two-fold Comforter,
under the figures of the Lamb and the Dove.
Let Thy merciful kindness, O Lord, be upon us,
like as we do put our trust in Thee.

4. Intercession

Let us beseech the Lord in peace,
for the heavenly peace,
and the salvation of our souls ;—
for the peace of the whole world ;
for the stability of God's holy Churches,
and the union of them all ;—
for this holy house,
and those who enter it with faith and reverence ;
for our holy Fathers,
the honourable Presbytery, the Diaconate in Christ,
and all, both Clergy and people ;—
for this holy retreat, and all the city and country,
and all the faithful who dwell therein ;—

for salubrious weather, fruitfulness of earth,
and peaceful times ;—
for voyagers, travellers,
those who are in sickness, toil, and captivity,
and for their salvation.
Aid, save, pity, and preserve them,
O God, in Thy grace.
Making mention
of the all-holy, undefiled, and more than blessed
Mary, Mother of God and Ever-Virgin,
with all saints,
let us commend ourselves, and each other,
and all our life,
to Christ our God.
To Thee, O Lord, for it is fitting,
be glory, honour, and worship.
The grace of our Lord, Jesus Christ,
and the love of God,
and the communion of the Holy Ghost,
be with me, and with all of us.   Amen.
I commend me and mine, and all that belongs to me,
to Him who is able to keep me without falling,
and to place me immaculate
before the presence of His glory,
to the only wise God and our Saviour ;

to whom be glory and greatness,
strength and authority,
both now and for all ages.   Amen.

5. Praise

O Lord, my Lord,
for my being, life, reason,
for nurture, protection, guidance,
for education, civil rights, religion,
for Thy gifts of grace, nature, fortune,
for redemption, regeneration, catechising,
for my call, recall, yea, many calls besides ;
for Thy forbearance, long-suffering,
long long-suffering
to me-ward,
many seasons, many years, up to this time ;
for all good things received, successes granted me,
good things done ;
for the use of things present,
for Thy promise, and my hope
of the enjoyment of good things to come ;
for my parents honest and good,
teachers kind,
benefactors never to be forgotten,
religious intimates congenial,

hearers thoughtful,
friends sincere,
domestics faithful,
for all who have advantaged me,
by writings, homilies, converse,
prayers, patterns, rebukes, injuries ;
for all these, and all others
which I know, which I know not,
open, hidden,
remembered, forgotten,
done when I wished, when I wished not,
I confess to Thee and will confess,
I bless Thee and will bless,
I give thanks to Thee and will give thanks,
all the days of my life.
Who am I, or what is my father's house,
that Thou shouldest look upon a dead dog,
the like of me ?
What reward shall I give unto the Lord
for all the benefits which He hath done unto me ?
What thanks can I recompense unto God,
for all He hath spared and borne with me until now ?
Holy, Holy, Holy,
worthy art Thou,
O Lord and our God, the Holy One,

to receive the glory, and the honour, and the power,
for Thou hast made all things,
and for Thy pleasure they are,
and were created.

The Sixth Day

Introduction

Early shall my prayer come before Thee.
Blessed art Thou, O Lord,
who broughtest forth of the earth, wild beasts, cattle,
and all the reptiles,
for food, clothing, help ;
and madest man after Thine image, to rule the earth,
and blessedst him.
The fore-counsel, fashioning hand,
breath of life, image of God,
appointment over the works,
charge to the Angels concerning him,
paradise.—
Heart, reins, eyes, ears, tongue, hands, feet,
life, sense, reason, spirit, free will,
memory, conscience,
the revelation of God, writing of the law,
oracles of prophets, music of psalms,

instruction of proverbs, experience of histories,
worship of sacrifices.

Blessed art Thou, O Lord,
for Thy great and precious promise
on this day,
concerning the Life-giving Seed,
and for its fulfilment in fulness of the times
on this day.

Blessed art Thou, O Lord,
for the holy Passion
of this day.
O by Thy salutary sufferings
on this day,
save us, O Lord.

1. Confession

I have withstood Thee, Lord,
but I return to Thee ;
for I have fallen by mine iniquity.
But I take with me words,
and I return unto Thee and say,
take away all iniquity and receive us graciously,
so will we render the calves of our lips.

Spare us, Lord, spare,
and give not Thine heritage to reproach,
to Thine enemies.

Lord, Lord, be propitious,
cease, I beseech Thee,
by whom shall Jacob arise?
for he is small.
Repent, O Lord, for this,
and this shall not be.

While observing lying vanities
I forsook my own mercy,
and am cast out of Thy sight.
When my soul fainted within me,
I remembered the Lord;
yet will I look again toward Thy Holy Temple;
Thou hast brought up my life from corruption.

Who is a God like unto Thee,
that pardoneth iniquity
to the remnant of His heritage?
He retaineth not His anger for ever,
because He delighteth in mercy.
Turn again and have compassion upon us, O Lord,
subdue our iniquities,

and cast all our sins into the depths of the sea,
according to Thy truth, and according to Thy mercy.

O Lord, I have heard Thy speech and was afraid,
in wrath remember mercy.
Behold me, Lord, clothed in filthy garments ;
behold Satan standing at my right hand ;
yet, O Lord, by the blood of Thy covenant,
by the fountain opened for sin and for uncleanness,
take away my iniquity,
and cleanse me from my sin.

Save me as a brand
plucked out of the fire.
Father, forgive me, for I knew not,
truly I knew not, what I did
in sinning against Thee.
Lord, remember me
when Thou comest in Thy kingdom.
Lord, lay not mine enemies' sins to their charge,
Lord, lay not my own to mine.
By Thy sweat bloody and clotted,
Thy soul in agony,
Thy head crowned with thorns, bruised with staves,
Thine eyes swimming with tears,

Thine ears full of insults,
Thy mouth moistened with vinegar and gall,
Thy face dishonourably stained with spitting,
Thy neck weighed down with the burden of the cross,
Thy back ploughed with the wheals and gashes
of the scourge,
Thy hands and feet stabbed through,
Thy strong cry, Eli, Eli,
Thy heart pierced with the spear,
the water and blood thence flowing,
Thy body broken,
Thy blood poured out,
Lord, forgive the offence of Thy servant,
and cover all his sins.
Turn away all Thy displeasure,
and turn Thyself from Thy wrathful indignation.
Turn me then, O God our Saviour,
and let Thine anger cease from us.
Wilt Thou be displeased at us for ever,
and stretch out Thy wrath from one generation
to another ?
Wilt Thou not turn again and quicken us,
that Thy people may rejoice in Thee ?
Shew us Thy mercy, O Lord,
and grant us Thy salvation.

2. Prayer for Grace

. . . .

the works of the flesh,
adultery, fornication, uncleanness, lasciviousness,
idolatry, witchcraft,
enmities, strifes,
emulations, heats,
quarrels, parties,
heresies, envyings, murders,
drunkennesses, revellings, and such like.

. . . .

the fruits of the Spirit,
love, joy, peace,
long-suffering, gentleness, goodness,
faith, meekness, temperance ;
the spirit of wisdom, of understanding,
of counsel, of might,
of knowledge, of godliness,
of fear of the Lord :—
and the gifts of the Spirit,
the word of wisdom, of knowledge,
faith, gifts of healing, working of miracles,
prophecy, discerning of spirits,
kinds of tongues, interpretation of tongues.

May Thy strong hand, O Lord[a],
　　be ever my defence ;
　　Thy mercy in Christ
　　　my salvation ;
　　Thy all-veritable word,
　　　my instructor ;
the grace of Thy life-bringing Spirit,
　　　my consolation
　　all along, and at last.
The Soul of Christ hallow me,
　and the Body strengthen me,
　and the Blood ransom me,
　and the Water wash me,
　and the Bruises heal me,
　and the Sweat refresh me,
　and the Wound hide me.
　　The peace of God
which passeth all understanding,
　keep my heart and thoughts
in the knowledge and the love of God.

3. Profession

I believe
that Thou hast created me ;

[a] Vide p. 146, edit. 1675.

despise not the work of Thine own hands ;—
that Thou madest me after Thine image and likeness,
suffer not Thy likeness to be blotted out ;—
that Thou hast redeemed me in Thy blood,
suffer not the cost of that redemption to perish ;
that Thou hast called me Christian after Thy name,
disdain not Thine own title ;
that Thou hast hallowed me in regeneration,
destroy not Thy holy work ;—
that Thou hast grafted me into the good olive-tree,
the member of a mystical body ;
the member of Thy mystical body
cut not off.
O think upon Thy servant as concerning Thy word,
wherein Thou hast caused me to put my trust.
My soul hath longed for Thy salvation,
and I have good hope because of Thy word.

4. Intercession

[I pray]
for the prosperous advance and good condition
of all the Christian army,
against the enemies of our most holy faith ;
for our holy fathers,
and all our brotherhood in Christ ;

for those who hate and those who love us,
for those who pity and those who minister to us ;
for those whom we have promised
to remember in prayer ;
for the liberation of captives ;
for our fathers and brethren absent ;
for those who voyage by sea ;
for those who lie in sickness.
Let us pray also for fruitfulness of the earth ;
and for every soul of orthodox Christians.
Let us bless pious kings,
orthodox high-priests,
the founders of this holy retreat,
our parents,
and all our forefathers
and our brethren departed.

5. Praise

Thou who, on man's transgressing Thy command,
and falling,
didst not pass him by, nor leave him, God of goodness;
but didst visit in ways manifold,
as a tender Father,
supplying him with Thy great and precious promise,
concerning the Life-giving Seed,

opening to him the door of faith,
and of repentance unto life,
and in fulness of the times,
sending Thy Christ Himself
to take on Him the seed of Abraham ;
and, in the oblation of His life,
to fulfil the Law's obedience ;
and, in the sacrifice of His death,
to take off the Law's curse ;
and, in His death,
to redeem the world ;
and, in His resurrection,
to quicken it :—
O Thou, who doest all things,
whereby to bring again our race to Thee,
that it may be partaker
of Thy divine nature and eternal glory ;
who hast borne witness
to the truth of Thy gospel
by many and various wonders,
in the ever-memorable converse of Thy saints,
in their supernatural endurance of torments,
in the overwhelming conversion of all lands
to the obedience of faith,
without might, or persuasion, or compulsion :—

Blessed be Thy Name,
and praised and celebrated,
and magnified, and high exalted,
and glorified, and hallowed ;
its record, and its memory,
and every memorial of it,
both now and for evermore.
Worthy art Thou to take the book,
and to open the seals thereof,
for Thou wast slain, and hast redeemed us to God
by Thy blood,
out of every kindred and tongue,
and people, and nation.
Worthy is the Lamb that was slain
to receive the power, and riches, and wisdom,
and strength, and honour, and glory, and blessing.
To Him that sitteth upon the Throne,
and to the Lamb,
be the blessing, and the honour, and the glory,
and the might,
for ever and ever.   Amen.
Salvation to our God, which sitteth upon the throne,
and to the Lamb.
Amen : the blessing and the glory and the wisdom,
and the thanksgiving and the honour,

and the power and the strength,
be unto our God,
for ever and ever,
Amen.

The Seventh Day

Introduction

O Lord, be gracious unto us,
we have waited for Thee ;
be Thou our arm every morning,
our salvation also in the time of trouble.
Blessed art Thou, O Lord,
who restedst on the seventh day
from all Thy works,
and blessedst and sanctifiedst it :
[concerning the Sabbath,
concerning the Christian rest instead of it,
concerning the burial of Christ,
and the resting from sin,
concerning those who are already gone to rest.]

1. Confession

I am ashamed, and blush, O my God,
to lift up my face to Thee,

for mine iniquities are increased
over my head,
and my trespass is grown up unto the heavens ;
since the days of youth
have I been in a great trespass
unto this day ;
I cannot stand before Thee because of this.
My sins are more in number than the sand of the sea,
my iniquities are multiplied,
and I not worthy to look up
and see the height of heaven,
from the number of my unrighteousnesses ;
and I have no relief,
because I have provoked Thine anger,
and done evil in Thy sight ;
not doing Thy will,
not keeping Thy commandments.
And now my heart kneels to Thee,
beseeching Thy goodness.
I have sinned, O Lord, I have sinned,
and I know mine iniquities ;
and I ask and beseech,
remit to me, O Lord, remit to me,
and destroy me not in mine iniquities ;
nor be Thou angry for ever,

nor reserve evil for me ;

nor condemn me

in the lowest parts of the earth.

Because Thou art God, the God of penitents,

and Thou shalt shew in me all Thy loving kindness ;

for Thou shalt save me unworthy,

according to Thy much pity,

and I will praise Thee alway.

Lord, if Thou wilt, Thou canst cleanse me ;

Lord, only say the word, and I shall be healed.

Lord, save me ;

Carest Thou not that we perish ?

Say to me, Be of good cheer, thy sins are remitted

to thee.

Jesu, Master, have mercy on me ;

Thou Son of David, Jesu, have mercy on me ;

Jesu, Son of David, Son of David.

Lord, say to me, Ephphatha.

Lord, I have no man[a] ;

Lord, say to me, Be loosed from thine infirmity.

Say unto my soul, I am thy salvation.

Say unto me, My grace is sufficient for thee.

Lord, how long wilt Thou be angry ?

shall Thy jealousy burn like fire for ever ?

[a] John v. 7.

O, remember not our old sins ;
but have mercy on us and that soon,
for we are come to great misery ;
Help us, O God of our salvation ;
for the glory of Thy Name.
O deliver us and be merciful unto our sins,
for Thy Name's sake.

2. Prayer for Grace

[O Lord, remit]
all my failings, shortcomings, falls,
offences, trespasses, scandals,
transgressions, debts, sins,
faults, ignorances, iniquities,
impieties, unrighteousnesses, pollutions.
The guilt of them,

be gracious unto,	pardon ;
remit,	forgive ;
be propitious unto,	spare ;
impute not,	charge not, remember not.

The stain,

pass by,	pass over ;
disregard,	overlook ;
hide,	wash away ;
blot out,	cleanse.

The hurt,

remit,   heal,   remedy ;

take off,   remove,   away with ;

abolish,   annul,   disperse, annihilate ;

that they be not found, that they exist not.

Supply

to faith,   virtue ;

to virtue,   knowledge ;

to knowledge,   continence ;

to continence,   patience ;

to patience,   godliness ;

to godliness,   brotherly love ;

to brotherly love,   charity.

That I forget not my cleansing from my former sins,

but give diligence to make my calling

and election sure

through good works.

3. Profession

I believe in Thee the Father ;

Behold then, if Thou a Father and we sons,

as a father pitieth sons,

be Thou of tender mercy towards us, O Lord.

I believe in Thee, the Lord ;

behold then, if Thou art Lord and we servants,

our eyes are upon Thee our Lord,
until Thou have mercy upon us.
I believe that though we be neither sons nor servants,
but dogs only,
yet we have leave to eat of the crumbs
that fall from Thy Table.
I believe that Christ is the Lamb of God ;
O Lamb of God that takest away the sins
of the world,
take Thou away mine.
I believe that Jesus Christ came into the world
to save sinners ;
Thou who camest to save sinners
save Thou me, of sinners
chief and greatest.
I believe that Christ came to save what was lost ;
Thou who camest to save the lost,
never suffer, O Lord, that to be lost which
Thou hast saved.
I believe that the Spirit is the Lord and Giver of life ;
Thou who gavest me a living soul,
give me that I receive not my soul in vain.
I believe that the Spirit gives grace
in His sacred things ;
give me that I receive not His grace in vain,

nor hope of His sacred things.
I believe that the Spirit intercedes for us
with plaints unutterable ;
grant me of His intercession and those plaints
to partake, O Lord.
Our fathers hoped in Thee,
they trusted in Thee, and Thou didst deliver them.
They called upon Thee and were holpen,
they put their trust in Thee, and were not confounded.
As Thou didst our fathers
in the generations of old,
so also deliver us, O Lord,
who trust in Thee.

4. Intercession

O Heavenly King,
confirm our faithful kings,
stablish the faith,
soften the nations,
pacify the world,
guard well this holy retreat,
and receive us in orthodox faith and repentance,
as a kind and loving Lord.
The power of the Father guide me,
the wisdom of the Son enlighten me,

the working of the Spirit quicken me.
Guard Thou my soul,
stablish my body,
elevate my senses,
direct my converse,
form my habits,
bless my actions,
fulfil my prayers,
inspire holy thoughts,
pardon the past,
correct the present,
prevent the future.

5. Praise

Now unto Him that is able to do
exceeding abundantly
above all that we ask or think,
according to the power that worketh in us,
to Him be glory
in the Church in Christ
unto all generations
world without end.   Amen.
Blessed, and praised, and celebrated,
and magnified, and exalted, and glorified,
and hallowed,

be Thy Name, O Lord,
its record, and its memory,
and every memorial of it ;
for the all-honourable senate of the Patriarchs,
the ever-venerable band of the Prophets,
the all-glorious college of the Apostles,
the Evangelists,
the all-illustrious army of the Martyrs,
the Confessors,
the assembly of Doctors,
the Ascetics,
the beauty of Virgins,
for Infants the delight of the world,—
for their faith, their hope,
their labours, their truth,
their blood, their zeal,
their diligence, their tears,
their purity, their beauty.
Glory to Thee, O Lord, glory to Thee,
glory to Thee who didst glorify them,
among whom we too glorify Thee.
Great and marvellous are Thy works,
Lord, the God Almighty ;
just and true are Thy ways,
O King of Saints.

Who shall not fear Thee, O Lord,
and glorify Thy Name ?
for Thou only art holy,
for all the nations shall come and worship
before Thee,
for Thy judgments are made manifest.
Praise our God, all ye His servants,
and ye that fear Him,
both small and great,
Alleluia,
for the Lord God Omnipotent reigneth ;
let us be glad and rejoice, and give honour to Him.
Behold the tabernacle of God is with men,
and He will dwell with them ;
and they shall be His people,
and God Himself shall be with them,
and shall wipe away all tears from their eyes.
And there shall be no more death ;
neither crying, neither pain any more,
for the former things are passed away.

Deprecations

I

O Lord [a], Thou knowest, and canst, and willest
the good of my soul.
Miserable man am I ;
I neither know, nor can, nor, as I ought,
will it.
Thou, O Lord, I beseech Thee,
in Thine ineffable affection,
so order concerning me,
and so dispose,
as Thou knowest to be most pleasing to Thee,
and most good for me.
[Thine is]
goodness, grace ;
love, kindness ;
benignity, gentleness, consideration ;
forbearance, long-suffering ;
much pity, great pity ;
mercies, multitude of mercies, yearnings of mercies ;

[a] Vide p. 92, edit. 1675.

kind yearnings, deep yearnings ;
in passing over,
in overlooking, in disregarding ;
many seasons, many years ;
[punishing] unwillingly, not willingly ;
not to the full,
not correspondently,
in wrath remembering mercy,
repenting of the evil,
compensating doubly,
ready to pardon,
to be reconciled,
to be appeased.

———

2

𝕷𝖎𝖙𝖆𝖓𝖞 [b]

Father, the Creator,
Son, the Redeemer,
Spirit, the Regenerator,
destroy me not,

[b] Page 180, edit. 1675.

whom Thou hast created, redeemed, regenerated.
Remember not, Lord, my sins,
nor the sins of my forefathers ;
neither take vengeance for our sins, theirs, nor mine.
Spare us, Lord, them and me,
spare Thy people,
and, among Thy people, Thy servant,
who is redeemed with Thy precious blood ;
and be not angry with us for ever.
Be merciful, be merciful ; spare us, Lord,
and be not angry with us for ever.
Be merciful, be merciful ; have pity on us, Lord,
and be not angry with us to the full.
Deal not, O Lord,
deal not with me after mine iniquities,
neither recompense me according to my sins ;
but after Thy great pity,
deal with me,
and according to the multitude of Thy mercies,
recompense me ;
after that so great pity,
and that multitude of mercies,
as Thou didst to our fathers
in the times of old ;—
by all that is dear unto Thee.

From all evil and adversity,
in all time of need ;
from this evil and this adversity,
in this time ;
raise me, rescue me, save me, O Lord.
Deliver me, O Lord,
and destroy me not.
On the bed of sickness ;
in the hour of death ;
in the day of judgment,
in that dreadful and fearful day,
rescue me, Lord, and save me ;—
from seeing the Judge's face overcast,
from being placed on the left,
from hearing the dreadful word, Depart from Me,
from being bound in chains of darkness,
from being cast into the outer darkness,
from being tormented in the pit of fire and brimstone,
where the smoke of the torments
ascendeth for ever.
Be merciful, be merciful,
spare us, pity us,
O Lord :
and destroy us not for ever,
deliver and save us.

Let it not be, O Lord ; and that it be not,

take away from me, O Lord,

hardness of heart,

desperateness after sinning,

blindness of heart,

contempt of Thy threats,

a cauterized conscience,

a reprobate mind,

the sin against the Holy Ghost,

the sin unto death,

the four crying sins [c] ;

the six which forerun [d]

the sin against the Holy Ghost.

Deliver me

from all ills and abominations of this world,

from plague, famine, and war ;

earthquake, flood, and fire,

the stroke of immoderate rain and drought,

blast and blight ;

thunder, lightning and tempest ;

epidemic sickness, acute and malignant,

unexpected death ;

[c] Wilful murder, the sin of Sodom, oppressing the poor, defrauding workmen of their wages.

[d] Despair of salvation, presumption of God's mercy, impugning known truth, envy at another's grace, obstinacy in sin, and impenitence.

from ills and difficulties in the Church,
from private interpretation,
from innovation in things sacred,
from heterodox teaching ;
from unhealthy enquiries and interminable disputes,
from heresies, schisms, scandals,
public and private,
from making gods of kings,
from flattering of the people,
from the indifference of Saul,
from the scorn of Michal,
from the greediness of Hophni,
from the plunder of Athaliah,
from the priesthood of Micah,
from the brotherhood of Simon and Judas,
from the doctrine of men unlearned
and unestablished,
from the pride of novices,
from the people resisting the priest :—
from ills and difficulties in the state,
from anarchy, many rulers, tyranny,
from Asher, Jeroboam, Rehoboam, Gallio, Haman,
the profligacy of Ahithophel,
the foolishness of Zoan [e],

[e] Isai. xix.

the statutes of Omri,
the justice of Jezebel,
the overflowings of Belial[f],
the courage of Peor,
the valley of Achor,
pollution of blood or seed,
incursion of enemies,
civil war,
bereavement of good governors,
accession of evil and unprincipled governors ;
from an intolerable life,
in despondence, sickness, ill-fame,
distress, peril, slavery, restlessness :
from death
in sin, shame, tortures,
desperateness, defilement, violence, treachery ;
from death unexpected,
from death eternal.

[f] Ps. xviii. 4.

Forms of Intercession

I [a]

For all creatures,
men,
persons compassed
with infirmity.
Churches
Catholic,
Eastern,
Western,
British.
The Episcopate,
Presbytery,
clergy,
Christian people.
States
of the whole earth,
Christian,

neighbouring,
our own.
Rulers,
kings,
religious kings,
our own.
councillors,
judges,
nobles,
soldiers,
sailors,
the people,
the rising generation,
schools,
those at court,
in cities,

[a] Vide p. 90, edit. 1675.

the country.
Those who serve
the soul ;
those who serve
the body,
in food,
clothing,
health,
necessaries.
[Those who have a claim
on my prayers,]
in nature,

by benefits,
from trust,
formerly or now,
in friendship,
in love,
in neighbourhood ;
from promise,
from mutual offices,
from want of leisure,
from destitution,
from extremity.

———

2 b

Thy whole creation,   the world,
our whole race,   the inhabited earth,
the states of the world,
the Catholic Church,   the Christian religion,
the separate Churches,
the separate states,
our Church,   our country,
our state,

b Vide p. 170, edit. 1675.

the orders in each,

the persons in the orders,   the priesthood,

the person of the king, of the prince,

the City,

the parish in which I was baptized,

All-Hallows, Barking,

My two schools,

my University,

my College,

the parish committed to me, St. Giles's,

the three Churches

of Southwell,

St. Paul's,

Westminster ;

the three Dioceses

of Chichester,

Ely,

Winton,

my home,

my kindred,

those who shew me pity,

those who minister to me ;

my neighbours,

my friends,

those who have a claim on me.

3^c

The creation,   the race of man,
all in affliction and in prosperity,
in error,   and in truth,
in sin,   and in grace ;
the Church Ecumenical,
Eastern, Western, our own,
Rulers, Clergy, people.
States of the earth,
Christian, neighbouring, our own,
the King, the Queen, the Prince,
the nobles.
Parliament, Law Courts, army, police.
The Commons,
farmers, merchants, artisans,
down to mean workmen,
and poor.
Those who have a claim on me,
from kindred,
benefaction,
ministration of things temporal,
charge formerly or now,

^c Vide p. 206, edit. 1675.

natural kindness,
Christian love,
neighbourhood,
promise on my part,
their own desire,
their lack of leisure,
sympathy for their extreme misery ;
any good work,
any noble action,
any scandal from me,
having none to pray for them.

4 [d]

World,	earth inhabited.
Church, throne,	kingdom, altar.
Council-chamber, schools,	law courts, work-places.
Infants, the grown,	boys, youths,

[d] Vide p. 210, edit. 1675.

men,   elderly,
aged,   decrepit.

The possessed,   weak-hearted,
sick,   prisoners,
orphans,   widows,
foreigners,
travellers,   voyagers,
with child,   who give suck,
in bitter bondage,   in desolateness,
overladen.

Meditations

I

On Christian Duty

What shall I do that I may inherit eternal life?
　Keep the commandments.　*Mark* x. 17.
What shall we do?
　Repent and be baptized every one of you.
　　　　　　　　　　　　　Acts ii. 37, 38.
What must I do to be saved?
　Believe on the Lord Jesus Christ.　*Acts* xvi. 31.
What shall we do then?
(To the multitude.) He who hath two coats, let him impart
　　　to him that hath none.
　He that hath meat, let him do likewise.
(To the publicans.) Exact no more than is appointed you.
(To soldiers.) Do violence to no man; neither accuse
　　any falsely; be content with your wages.
　　　　　　　　　　　　Luke iii. 10–14.

The knowledge and faith
of [God's] justice   [God's] mercy,
[leads] unto

fear,	hope,
abasement,	consolation,
repentance,	thanksgiving,
fasting,	almsgiving,
prayers,	hymns,
patience,	obedience,
a sacrifice.	an oblation.

2

On the Day of Judgment

Father Unoriginate, Only-begotten Son,
Life-giving Spirit,
merciful, pitiful, long-suffering,
full of pity, full of kind yearnings,
who lovest the just and pitiest the sinful,
who passest by sins and grantest petitions,
God of penitents,
Saviour of sinners,
I have sinned before Thee, O Lord,

and thus and thus have I done.

Alas, alas ! woe, woe.

How was I enticed by my own lust !

How I hated instruction !

Nor felt I fear nor shame

at Thy incomprehensible glory,

Thy awful presence,

Thy fearful power,

Thy exact justice,

Thy winning goodness.

I will call if there be any that will answer me ;

to which of the saints shall I turn ?

O wretched man that I am,

who shall deliver me from the body of this death ?

how fearful is Thy judgment, O Lord ?

when the thrones are set

and Angels stand around,

and men are brought in,

the books opened,

the works enquired into,

the thoughts examined,

and the hidden things of darkness.

What judgment shall be upon me ?

who shall quench my flame ?

who shall lighten my darkness,

if Thou pity me not ?
Lord, as Thou art loving,
give me tears,
give me floods, give me to-day.
For then will be the incorruptible Judge,
the horrible judgment-seat,
the answer without excuses,
the inevitable charges,
the shameful punishment,
the endless Gehenna,
the pitiless Angels,
the yawning hell,
the roaring stream of fire,
the unquenchable flame,
the dark prison,
the rayless darkness,
the bed of live coals,
the unwearied worm,
the indissoluble chains,
the bottomless chaos,
the impassable wall,
the inconsolable cry,
none to stand by me,
none to plead for me,
none to snatch me out.

But I repent, Lord, O Lord, I repent,
help Thou mine impenitence,
and more, and still more,
pierce, rend, crush my heart.
Behold, O Lord, that I am
indignant with myself,
for my senseless, profitless,
hurtful, perilous passions;
that I loathe myself,
for these inordinate, unseemly,
deformed, insincere,
shameful, disgraceful
passions,
that my confusion is daily before me,
and the shame of my face hath covered me.
Alas! woe, woe—
O me, how long?
Behold, Lord, that I sentence myself
to punishment everlasting,
yea, and all miseries of this world.
Behold me, Lord, self-condemned;
Behold, Lord, and enter not into judgment
with Thy servant.
And now, Lord,
I humble myself under Thy mighty hand,

I bend to Thee, O Lord, my knees,
I fall on my face to the earth.
Let this cup pass from me !
I stretch forth my hands unto Thee ;
I smite my breast, I smite on my thigh.
Out of the deep my soul crieth unto Thee,
as a thirsty land ;
and all my bones,
and all that is within me.
Lord, hear my voice.

3

On Human Frailness

Have mercy on me, Lord, for I am weak ;
remember, Lord, how short my time is ;
remember that I am but flesh,
a wind that passeth away, and cometh not again.
My days are as grass, as a flower of the field ;
for the wind goeth over me, and I am gone,
and my place shall know me no more.
I am dust and ashes,
earth and grass,

flesh and breath,

corruption and the worm,

a stranger upon the earth,

dwelling in a house of clay,

few and evil my days,

to-day, and not to-morrow,

in the morning, yet not until night,

in a body of sin,

in a world of corruption,

of few days, and full of trouble,

coming up, and cut down like a flower,

and as a shadow, having no stay.

Remember this, O Lord, and suffer, remit ;

what profit is there in my blood,

when I go down to the pit ?

By the multitude of Thy mercies,

by the riches and excessive redundance

of Thy pity ;

by all that is dear to Thee,

all that we should plead,

and before and beyond all things, by Thyself,

by Thyself, O Lord, and by Thy Christ.

Lord, have mercy upon me, the chief of sinners.

O my Lord, let Thy mercy rejoice

against Thy judgment in my sin.

O Lord, hear, O Lord, forgive,
O Lord, hearken,
O Lord, hearken and do,
do and defer not for Thine own sake,
defer not, O Lord my God.

For Holy Communion

O Lord,
I am not worthy, I am not fit,
that Thou shouldest come under the roof
of my soul ;
for it is all desolate and ruined ;
nor hast Thou in me fitting place
to lay Thy head.
But, as Thou didst vouchsafe
to lie in the cavern and manger of brute cattle,
as Thou didst not disdain
to be entertained in the house of Simon the leper,
as Thou didst not disdain
that harlot, like me, who was a sinner,
coming to Thee and touching Thee ;
as Thou abhorredst not
her polluted and loathsome mouth ;
nor the thief upon the cross
confessing Thee :

So me too the ruined, wretched,
and excessive sinner,
deign to receive to the touch and partaking
of the immaculate, supernatural, life-giving,
and saving mysteries
of Thy all-holy Body
and Thy precious Blood.
Listen, O Lord, our God,
from Thy holy habitation,
and from the glorious throne of Thy kingdom,
and come to sanctify us.
O Thou who sittest on high with the Father,
and art present with us here invisibly ;
come Thou to sanctify the gifts which lie before Thee,
and those in whose behalf, and by whom,
and the things for which,
they are brought near Thee.
And grant to us communion,
unto faith, without shame,
love without dissimulation,
fulfilment of Thy commandments,
alacrity for every spiritual fruit ;
hindrance of all adversity,
healing of soul and body ;
that we too, with all Saints,

who have been well-pleasing to Thee from the
beginning,
may become partakers
of Thy incorrupt and everlasting goods,
which Thou hast prepared, O Lord, for them that
love Thee ;
in whom Thou art glorified
for ever and ever.
Lamb of God,
that takest away the sin of the world,
take away the sin of me,
the utter sinner.

[Unto a pledge of communion. *Acts* ii. 42.
A memorial of the Dispensation. *Eph.* iii. 2.
A showing forth of His death. 1 *Cor.* xi. 26.
A communion of Body and Blood. *Luke* xxii. 19.
A sharing in the Spirit. 1 *Cor.* xii. 13.
Remission of sins. *Matt.* xxvi. 28.
A riddance of things contrary. 1 *Cor.* v. 7.
Rest of conscience. *Matt.* xi. 29.
Blotting out of debts. *Col.* ii. 14.
Cleansing of stains. *Heb.* ix. 14.
Healing of the soul's sicknesses. 1 *Pet.* ii. 24.
Renewing of the covenant. *Psalm* ii. 5.
Food of spiritual life. *John* vi. 27.

Increase of strengthening grace. *Heb.* xiii. 9.

And of winning consolation. *Luke* ii. 25.

Compunction of penitence. 2 *Cor.* vii. 9.

Illumination of mind. *Luke* xxiv. 31.

Exercise of humility. 1 *Peter* v. 5.

Seal of faith. 2 *Cor.* i. 22.

Fulness of wisdom. *Rom.* xi. 33.

Bond of love. *John* xiii. 35.

Call for a collection. 1 *Cor.* xvi. 1.

A means of endurance. 1 *Peter* iv. 1.

Liveliness of thanksgiving. *Psalm* cxvi. 12.

Confidence of prayer. *Ibid.* 13.

Mutual indwelling. *John* vi. 56.

Pledge of the resurrection. *Ibid.* 34.

Acceptable defence in judgment. *Luke* xiv. 18.

Covenant of the inheritance. *Luke* xxii. 20.

Figure of perfection. *John* xvii. 23.]

We then remembering, O sovereign Lord,
    in the presence of Thy holy mysteries,
        the salutary passion of Thy Christ,
            His life-giving cross,
                most precious death,
                three days' sepulture,
                resurrection from the dead,
                ascent into heaven,

session at the right hand of Thee, the Father,
His fearful and glorious coming ;
we beseech Thee, O Lord,
that we, receiving in the pure testimony
of our conscience,
our portion of Thy sacred things,
may be made one with the holy Body and Blood
of Thy Christ ;
and receiving them not unworthily,
we may hold Christ indwelling in our hearts,
and may become a temple
of Thy Holy Spirit.
Yea, O our God,
nor make any of us guilty
of Thy dreadful and heavenly mysteries,
nor infirm in soul or body
from partaking of them unworthily.
But grant us
until our last and closing breath
worthily to receive a hope of Thy holy things,
for sanctification, enlightening, strengthening,
a relief of the weight of my many sins,
a preservative against all satanic working,
a riddance and hindrance of my evil conscience,
a mortification of my passions,

an appropriation of Thy commandments,
an increase of Thy divine grace ;
and a securing of Thy kingdom.

* * * * * *

It is finished and done,
so far as in our power,
Christ our God,
the mystery of Thy dispensation.
For we have held remembrance of Thy death,
we have seen the figure of Thy resurrection,
we have been filled with Thy endless life,
we have enjoyed Thy uncloying dainties,
which graciously vouchsafe all of us,
in the world to come.
Lord, the good God,
pardon every soul,
that purifieth his heart to seek God,
the Lord God of his fathers,
though he be not cleansed
according to the purification of the sanctuary.